P9-AQR-739

The Duty to
Rescue

CRIME, JUSTICE, AND PUNISHMENT

The Duty to Rescue

Rose Blue and
Corinne J. Naden

Austin Sarat, GENERAL EDITOR

CHELSEA HOUSE PUBLISHERS
Philadelphia

Frontis: *A painting depicting the Good Samaritan story, by British artist Joseph Highmore (1744).*

Chelsea House Publishers

Editor in Chief Stephen Reginald
Managing Editor James D. Gallagher
Production Manager Pamela Loos
Art Director Sara Davis
Director of Photography Judy L. Hasday
Senior Production Editor LeeAnne Gelletly

Staff for THE DUTY TO RESCUE

Senior Editor John Ziff
Associate Art Director/Designer Takeshi Takahashi
Picture Researcher Sandy Jones
Cover Illustrator Janet Hamlin

First Printing

1 3 5 7 9 8 6 4 2

The Chelsea House World Wide Web address is
http://www.chelseahouse.com

Library of Congress Cataloging-in-Publication Data

Blue, Rose.
The duty to rescue / Rose Blue and Corinne J. Naden;
Austin Sarat, general editor.
    p. cm. — (Crime, justice, and punishment)
Includes bibliographical references and index.
Summary: Examines what happens when a crime is perpe-
trated against an innocent person and nobody cares, dis-
cussing the protection of those responsible for rescuing vic-
tims and the legal aspects of such situations, in the United
States, overseas, in the air, and on the water.

ISBN 0-7910-4286-3

1. Emergency assistance—United States—Juvenile literature. 2. Victims of crimes—United States—Popular works.
[1. Victims of crimes. 2. Violent crimes. 3. Crime.] I.
Naden, Corinne J. II. Sarat, Austin. III. Title. IV. Series.
KF1329.Z9B58 1999
362.88—dc21
                                        99-38448
                                            CIP

Contents

2.95

CRIME, JUSTICE, AND PUNISHMENT

CAPITAL PUNISHMENT

CHILDREN, VIOLENCE, AND MURDER

CLASSIC CONS AND SWINDLES

CRIMES AGAINST CHILDREN:
CHILD ABUSE AND NEGLECT

CRIMES AGAINST HUMANITY

CYBER CRIMES

DETERRENCE AND REHABILITATION

DRUGS, CRIME,
AND CRIMINAL JUSTICE

THE DUTY TO RESCUE

ESPIONAGE AND TREASON

THE FBI'S MOST WANTED

FORENSIC SCIENCE

THE GRAND JURY

GREAT PROSECUTIONS

HATE CRIMES

HIGH CRIMES AND MISDEMEANORS

INFAMOUS TRIALS

THE INSANITY DEFENSE

JUDGES AND SENTENCING

THE JURY SYSTEM

JUVENILE CRIME

MAJOR UNSOLVED CRIMES

ORGANIZED CRIME

POLICE AND POLICING

PRISONS

PRIVATE INVESTIGATORS
AND BOUNTY HUNTERS

RACE, CRIME, AND PUNISHMENT

REVENGE AND RETRIBUTION

RIGHTS OF THE ACCUSED

SERIAL MURDER

TERRORISM

VICTIMS AND VICTIMS' RIGHTS

WHITE-COLLAR CRIME

Fears and Fascinations:

An Introduction to Crime, Justice, and Punishment

By Austin Sarat

We live with crime and images of crime all around us. Crime evokes in most of us a deep aversion, a feeling of profound vulnerability, but it also evokes an equally deep fascination. Today, in major American cities the fear of crime is a major fact of life, some would say a disproportionate response to the realities of crime. Yet the fear of crime is real, palpable in the quickened steps and furtive glances of people walking down darkened streets. At the same time, we eagerly follow crime stories on television and in movies. We watch with a "who done it" curiosity, eager to see the illicit deed done, the investigation undertaken, the miscreant brought to justice and given his just deserts. On the streets the presence of crime is a reminder of our own vulnerability and the precariousness of our taken-for-granted rights and freedoms. On television and in the movies the crime story gives us a chance to probe our own darker motives, to ask "Is there a criminal within?" as well as to feel the collective satisfaction of seeing justice done.

Fear and fascination, these two poles of our engagement with crime, are, of course, only part of the story. Crime is, after all, a major social and legal problem, not just an issue of our individual psychology. Politicians today use our fear of, and fascination with, crime for political advantage. How we respond to crime, as well as to the political uses of the crime issue, tells us a lot about who we are as a people as well as what we value and what we tolerate. Is our response compassionate or severe? Do we seek to understand or to punish, to enact an angry vengeance or to rehabilitate and welcome the criminal back into our midst? The CRIME, JUSTICE, AND PUNISHMENT series is designed to explore these themes, to ask why we are fearful and fascinated, to probe the meanings and motivations of crimes and criminals and of our responses to them, and, finally, to ask what we can learn about ourselves and the society in which we live by examining our responses to crime.

Crime is always a challenge to the prevailing normative order and a test of the values and commitments of law-abiding people. It is sometimes a Raskolnikov-like act of defiance, an assertion of the unwillingness of some to live according to the rules of conduct laid out by organized society. In this sense, crime marks the limits of the law and reminds us of law's all-too-regular failures. Yet sometimes there is more desperation than defiance in criminal acts; sometimes they signal a deep pathology or need in the criminal. To confront crime is thus also to come face-to-face with the reality of social difference, of class privilege and extreme deprivation, of race and racism, of children neglected, abandoned, or abused whose response is to enact on others what they have experienced themselves. And occasionally crime, or what is labeled a criminal act, represents a call for justice, an appeal to a higher moral order against the inadequacies of existing law.

Figuring out the meaning of crime and the motivations of criminals and whether crime arises from defiance, desperation, or the appeal for justice is never an easy task. The motivations and meanings of crime are as varied as are the persons who engage in criminal conduct. They are as mysterious as any of the mysteries of the human soul. Yet the desire to know the secrets of crime and the criminal is a strong one, for in that knowledge may lie one step on the road to protection, if not an assurance of one's own personal safety. Nonetheless, as strong as that desire may be, there is no available technology that can allow us to know the whys of crime with much confidence, let alone a scientific certainty. We can, however, capture something about crime by studying the defiance, desperation, and quest for justice that may be associated with it. Books in the CRIME, JUSTICE, AND PUNISHMENT series will take up that challenge. They tell stories of crime and criminals, some famous, most not, some glamorous and exciting, most mundane and commonplace.

This series will, in addition, take a sober look at American criminal justice, at the procedures through which we investigate crimes and identify criminals, at the institutions in which innocence or guilt is determined. In these procedures and institutions we confront the thrill of the chase as well as the challenge of protecting the rights of those who defy our laws. It is through the efficiency and dedication of law enforcement that we might capture the criminal; it is in the rare instances of their corruption or brutality that we feel perhaps our deepest betrayal. Police, prosecutors, defense lawyers, judges, and jurors administer criminal justice and in their daily actions give substance to the guarantees of the Bill of Rights. What is an adversarial system of justice? How does it work? Why do we have it? Books in the CRIME, JUSTICE, AND PUNISHMENT series will examine the thrill of the chase as we seek to capture the criminal. They will also reveal the drama and majesty of the criminal trial as well as the day-to-day reality of a criminal justice system in which trials are the exception and negotiated pleas of guilty are the rule.

When the trial is over or the plea has been entered, when we have separated the innocent from the guilty, the moment of punishment has arrived. The injunction to punish the guilty, to respond to pain inflicted by inflicting pain, is as old as civilization itself. "An eye for an eye and a tooth for a tooth" is a biblical reminder that punishment must measure pain for pain. But our response to the criminal must be better than and different from the crime itself. The biblical admonition, along with the constitutional prohibition of "cruel and unusual punishment," signals that we seek to punish justly and to be just not only in the determination of who can and should be punished, but in how we punish as well. But neither reminder tells us what to do with the wrongdoer. Do we rape the rapist, or burn the home of the arsonist? Surely justice and decency say no. But, if not, then how can and should we punish? In a world in which punishment is neither identical to the crime nor an automatic response to it, choices must be made and we must make them. Books in the CRIME, JUSTICE, AND PUNISHMENT series will examine those choices and the practices, and politics, of punishment. How do we punish and why do we punish as we do? What can we learn about the rationality and appropriateness of today's responses to crime by examining our past and its responses? What works? Is there, and can there be, a just measure of pain?

CRIME, JUSTICE, AND PUNISHMENT brings together books on some of the great themes of human social life. The books in this series capture our fear and fascination with crime and examine our responses to it. They remind us of the deadly seriousness of these subjects. They bring together themes in law, literature, and popular culture to challenge us to think again, to think anew, about subjects that go to the heart of who we are and how we can and will live together.

*   *   *   *   *

What is the relationship of law and morality? Are there areas where law can and should reflect our moral intuitions? Or, is it better if the legal world and the moral world remain separate? These questions are as vexing as any that engage the attention of students of law. Going back at least as far as the debate between John Austin and William Blackstone, so-called natural law theorists have argued that there is a necessary and important connection between law and morals and that immoral law is not law at all. Legal positivists, on the other hand, see no *necessary* connection. Up to the present day, the phrase "legislating morality" evokes in many the fear of having their freedom limited to satisfy the moral beliefs of others. And, it is one thing to be required to follow a set of beliefs or practices to which one does not subscribe. But it is quite another to be punished for failing to take morally praiseworthy action.

It is this last issue that is at the heart of the discussion of the duty to rescue. Traditionally the law did not impose a duty to come to the aid of persons in distress except in very narrow circumstances. While recognizing a clear moral duty to rescue, courts argued that persons should be legally free to follow or to ignore, as their conscience dictated, what morality required.

The Duty to Rescue provides a compelling examination of the complex relations of law and morality. It describes a world of indifferent strangers, everyone leaving everyone else to fend for themselves, and recent legal efforts to change this attitude. It traces legislative efforts to encourage Good Samaritans, or at least to protect them from adverse legal consequences. As the authors remind us, "It's not always easy to see where responsibility or morality lies when the subject of the duty to rescue comes up." Yet they also show how the American attitude is anomalous. Many other countries impose a legal duty to rescue. In the end, they rightly remind us that the future of the duty to rescue in this country may be very different from its past.

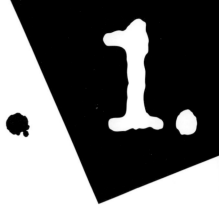

WHAT HAPPENS WHEN NOBODY CARES?

Kitty Genovese, stabbed on three separate occasions over the course of a half hour, finally died at the door of this apartment building in Queens, New York. What shocked the nation more than the brutality of the 1964 murder was the reaction of Genovese's neighbors: 38 people had seen or heard the attack, but none had done anything to come to her aid.

The street was dark and quiet that early morning in March 1964. It was 3:20 A.M. Catherine Genovese—everyone called her Kitty—was just getting home from her bartending job. She locked her car and began to walk the short distance to her apartment building in the borough of Queens, New York City.

In the stillness of predawn, it might have seemed to Kitty that she was the only person awake in that residential, middle-class neighborhood. Unfortunately, she wasn't. As she neared her building, a man grabbed her. He had a knife.

Kitty Genovese screamed for help, shouting that she was being stabbed. Someone turned on a light, opened a window, and called for quiet. The man disappeared and the light went out. Kitty struggled to get to her building, but the man returned from the shadows and stabbed her again.

Once more she screamed, this time calling out that

she was dying. More lights went on and more windows opened. Once again, the killer left the scene. Kitty Genovese crawled to the back of her apartment building to hide. But the man followed and attacked for the third and final time, fatally wounding her.

Over the course of half an hour, while Kitty Genovese was being stabbed on three separate occasions, not one of the 38 people who either heard or watched the murder did anything to help her. They didn't attempt to stop the killer even by shouting, let alone coming to Kitty's rescue. Worst of all, they didn't even pick up the telephone and call the police.

Finally, at 3:50 A.M., Kitty's next-door neighbor did make a phone call. The police were on the scene in two minutes. If they had been alerted at 3:20 A.M., Kitty Genovese might be alive today.

Why didn't her neighbor call earlier? Why didn't *anyone* call earlier? Most said they just didn't want to get involved. In fact, her neighbor decided to call only after he thought about it for a long while and then called a friend to see if that was the *right* thing to do!

The killer, 29-year-old Winston Moseley, was arrested six days later. Married, with two children and a home in Queens, he had no previous criminal record. However, he did confess to two other murders, one a month earlier, the other the preceding summer. Both victims were women. Moseley was given a sentence of 20 years to life. He is still in prison.

Anyone who was old enough to read a newspaper in 1964 is likely to remember the horrible, and probably preventable, death of Kitty Genovese. It's still talked about today whenever conversation centers on a person's duty to help another in danger. For a long time after that shocking murder, people said things like "Why didn't her neighbors help?" "How could they just let her die?" "What kind of monsters would do nothing?" "There ought to be a law!"

But in most states, there is no law. As an American

Overhead photo showing the Genovese murder scene. After parking her car (1) and walking toward her apartment, Genovese was stabbed on the sidewalk (2). When she screamed and someone shouted out a window, her assailant left. She staggered around the corner, but the attacker returned and stabbed her again (3). Genovese screamed that she was dying, lights went on in windows, and the killer again left. She crawled to the back of her apartment building to hide (4), but the attacker found her there and killed her.

citizen, in most states you have no duty to rescue someone from harm. It's not against the law to stand by and let someone be stabbed, raped, or beaten to death. We might question the lack of compassion or morality on the part of Kitty Genovese's New York neighbors, but we can't question their legal right to do what they did—or rather, not do what they could have done.

It may be legal not to perform a duty of rescue, but should it be? Should the laws of a government punish people for *not* doing what they should do, or should we punish only for *doing* something wrong?

John Stuart Mill, the noted British philosopher and economist of the 19th century, had some ideas about that. One of his most famous works is an 1859 essay entitled "On Liberty." In it Mill declared that no government had the right to interfere with an individual's freedom of action—or liberty—unless that freedom was in itself a danger to society. Said Mill, "The only purpose for which power can be rightfully exercised over any member of a civilized community, against his will, is to prevent harm to others." In personal concerns, Mill said, the individual's "independence is, of right, absolute. Over himself, over his own body and mind, the individual is sovereign." Then, to make himself perfectly clear, Mill stated that "the only freedom which deserves the name, is that of pursuing our own good in our own way, so long as we do not attempt to deprive others of theirs, or impede their efforts to obtain it."

Mill's widely reviewed essay was an immediate success. However, many people expressed the fear that such views of government and the individual could lead to an excess of selfish actions.

Even if, as Mill might argue, we cannot or should not insist that an individual come to another's rescue, many people would argue that there is a *moral* duty to do so. In most countries, failing to help a person in peril has always been considered a very serious moral offense.

This moral duty is mentioned in the Bible. In the Gospel of Luke (10:29–37), Jesus tells the story of the Good Samaritan. After two travelers, one a priest, ignore an injured man by the side of the road, he is helped by a compassionate Samaritan, who takes the man to an inn and nurses him back to health. So grew the concept of the Good Samaritan, a person willing to help even strangers who are in distress.

From biblical days to modern times, the question of helping or not helping our neighbors hasn't gone away. More than three decades after the tragedy of Kitty Genovese, the behavior of our fellow citizens was very much back in the news. This time a seven-year-old girl died, and once again no one seemed to care. It happened in the early morning hours of May 25, 1997, at the Primadonna Casino (now the Primm Valley Resort and Casino) near Las Vegas, Nevada. Two 18-year-olds from California, Jeremy Strohmeyer and David Cash

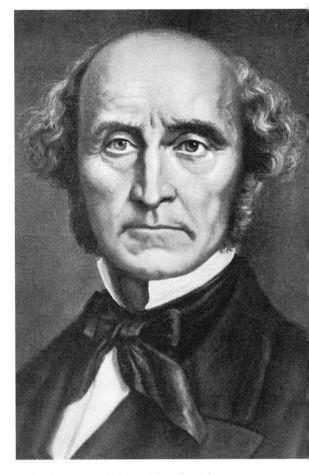

British philosopher John Stuart Mill. In an 1859 essay titled "On Liberty," Mill argued that the state can legitimately interfere with an individual's freedom of action only to prevent the individual from harming others. By implication citizens cannot, in Mill's view, be compelled to rescue people in distress.

Jr., were growing bored as they waited for David's father to leave the poker table. Jeremy began playing tag in the casino arcade with little Sherrice Iverson. Like the teenagers, Sherrice, along with her 14-year-old half-brother Harold, was waiting for her father, Leroy Iverson, to finish gambling. He had given Sherrice and Harold money to play in the arcade.

Harold didn't notice when Sherrice skipped into the ladies room at 3:47 A.M., but Jeremy Strohmeyer did. He followed her.

David Cash saw his friend follow Sherrice into the ladies room, and he went in after them. He watched the child struggle as Strohmeyer grabbed her and began

Protesters at the University of California at Berkeley ask why David Cash is allowed to attend the school. The answer: Even though his failure to prevent or report the murder of Sherrice Iverson was reprehensible, he broke no laws.

sexually molesting her. Later he said that he told Strohmeyer to let her go. After about two minutes, Cash left the rest room and waited for his friend to come out. When Strohmeyer appeared about 20 minutes later, Cash asked what had happened. Strohmeyer said, "I killed her." After sexually molesting her, he had twisted the little girl's neck until she died.

A hidden video security camera in the rest room eventually led the police to Jeremy Strohmeyer, who at first pleaded not guilty. In September of 1998, facing a possible death sentence, he confessed to the murder and will spend the rest of his life in prison, without parole.

David Cash did not try to stop the attack on Sherrice Iverson. He did not try to stop the murder. Nor did he tell anyone what he had seen in the rest room at the casino. After a summer of notorious publicity, he entered the University of California at Berkeley that fall. When asked why he hadn't turned Strohmeyer in to the police, Cash replied, "I didn't want to be the person who takes away his last day of freedom." When asked if he was appalled at his friend's actions, Cash said, "I'm not going to lose sleep over somebody else's problems."

After the tragedy, both of Sherrice's parents, who were separated, filed a wrongful-death lawsuit against the casino and Jeremy Strohmeyer. In turn, the casino filed its own lawsuit—against Jeremy Strohmeyer, David Cash, and Sherrice Iverson's father. The actions of all three, contended the casino, contributed to the death of the child.

Most people would surely find David Cash's non-action and his attitude reprehensible. Most would also question the lack of responsible supervision by the murdered girl's father. Many might agree that both men are at least partly responsible for the little girl's death. But Nevada authorities decided not to charge Leroy Iverson with child neglect. As for David Cash, he has committed no crime, and he is free. But should he be? Should he be held responsible for not trying to stop an assault and murder? Should the law proclaim that it was his duty to rescue Sherrice Iverson?

Some people will say yes to these questions. But others will argue that it's not advisable, or even possible, to legislate morality. How, they ask, could that be done without infringing on a person's individual freedom and civil rights? We are not our brother's keeper, they say. We can't *make* someone care about someone else.

These are some of the issues explored in this book. In the end, perhaps, we all have to decide for ourselves if we want to be Good Samaritans and if we have a duty to rescue.

PROTECTING THE PROTECTOR

If you were asked whose duty it is to protect you from criminals, you would most likely answer "the police." And you would be wrong! Strange as it may sound, police officers have no duty to rescue or to protect a particular individual. They have, instead, a general duty to enforce the laws. Remember that a limited number of police are protecting a much larger number of citizens. It would be impractical to require them legally to rescue everyone who thinks he or she needs help. Instead, the police must be able to make judgments about which people need their immediate aid and which don't.

American courts have consistently accepted the view that the duty of the police to protect individuals is very limited. One important case from 1968, *Riss v. City of New York*, concerned a young woman, Linda Riss, who sought police protection because her ex-boyfriend (who had a criminal record) had repeatedly threatened her. The police did nothing. One day, someone hired by her boyfriend threw lye in Riss's face, blinding her in one eye. She sued the city of New York for not protecting her. Riss lost the case, however, because the court found that New York City police had no legal duty to protect her or any other particular individual.

In the Riss case, the danger had been fairly general—the former boyfriend had issued numerous threats before the lye attack. In the 1975 case of *Hartzler v. City of San Jose,* on the other hand, the threat was immediate and specific. Ruth Bunnell of San Jose, California, called police and asked them to protect her from her estranged husband, who had just called her and announced that he was coming to kill her. The police responded by telling Bunnell to call them when her husband arrived. She didn't get that chance, because when he arrived he stabbed her to death. Bunnell's estate sued. Once again, however, the court ruled that the police could not be held liable for failing to protect an individual. State and local police departments have no legal duty to help any given person.

This is not, of course, to say that police don't help individual people. Indeed they do, all the time. But it might be a good idea for citizens to remember that the job of their local police is not exactly what they think it is.

Besides looking to police for protection, people also look to neighbors and friends in time of trouble. After the tragedy of Kitty Genovese in 1964, many people asked why her neighbors seemed so unconcerned. Numerous newspaper reports and studies examined the incident. The University of Chicago Law School held a conference that focused on the behavior of the Good Samaritan and the Bad Samaritan, "The Law and Morality of Volunteering in Situations of Peril, or of Failing to Do So." In 1966 the American Psychological Association pondered the problem of the "unconcerned bystander." Maybe there was a way, people thought, to turn the unconcerned bystander into a concerned bystander—a Good Samaritan.

According to the ancient tale of the Good Samaritan, coming to the aid of a stranger in distress is a moral and noble act. But through the years, a sort of anti–Good Samaritan general rule had developed in the United States. It said that noble or not, a person has no legal duty to help another. In fact, in some cases people have actually been prosecuted or sued for playing the Good Samaritan. For instance, suppose Jack stops to help Joe, a stranger who is choking on a chicken bone. While applying sudden upward pressure to Joe's abdomen with his fist (the Heimlich maneuver), Jack succeeds in dislodging the bone but breaks two of Joe's ribs. Though saved from possible death, Joe decides to sue Jack for the broken ribs.

Obviously, when their reward might be legal trouble, not many people will want to offer help in an emergency. For this reason states have enacted so-called Good Samaritan laws. These laws differ from duty to rescue laws, which say that a person *must* offer at least reasonable help to someone in distress. A Good Samaritan law is intended to protect the protector from criminal prosecution or a civil lawsuit. In other words, a Good Samaritan law would protect Jack from being sued for breaking Joe's ribs. For example, in 1997 New York State passed a statute that protected veterinarians who volunteered aid to ill or injured animals. If the animal died, the vet could not be sued unless it could be proven that the medical help offered was grossly incompetent or negligent. This was followed by similar protection to all people who come to the aid of injured or ill individuals, including those who care for ill or disabled patients in their homes.

New York has also passed a number of laws that protect the volunteer who gives aid in an emergency, unless that aid is given in a "negligent, reckless, wanton, or willful manner." The Education Law covers registered nurses and licensed practical nurses as well as licensed physical therapists, physicians, and dentists. The Public Health Law protects volunteer ambulance and emergency medical technicians and people who offer aid to victims choking in a restaurant. The Executive Law covers those who come to the aid of a crime victim. The Transportation Law protects public transportation employees who help people in trouble on buses, trains, and the like. Ski patrol members are protected against being sued for the medical assistance they might give to ski accident victims.

Minnesota passed a statute that protects school bus drivers if they give emergency care. In Nevada and other states, this applies as well to ambulance drivers and firefighters. Massachusetts protects teachers, principals, and other school officials who give emergency first aid or transportation to a student who is injured in the building or on the grounds.

Since 1959 all 50 states have adopted some sort of Good Samaritan law to protect doctors and others when treating an injured party at the scene of an accident. Lawmakers understood that if people feared being sued for helping an accident victim, for instance, not many would be willing to give emergency aid. So the Good Samaritan laws protect the protector from the threat of liability for any damage done when giving assistance. However—and this is a big point—the assistance given must be reasonable.

Here are two examples. George is skiing alone in a remote area of a northern state. In a small clearing he spies Harry, sprawled unconscious in the snow. George doesn't know what happened, but he decides that he can't leave the man to die in the below-freezing temperature. He hauls Harry down the mountain, where the injured man receives first aid. George may have saved Harry's life, but what he didn't know was that the fall that knocked Harry unconscious also broke a bone in his back. By moving him, George made the injury worse. Now Harry is paralyzed. Can Harry sue

A firefighter and a paramedic treat a construction worker injured when the house he was working on collapsed. The victim's coworkers, seen in the background, were the first to come to his aid and are shielded from liability by Good Samaritan laws—provided the assistance they gave was reasonable.

Rescuing an injured cross-country skier. By definition emergencies require urgent action, often under less-than-ideal conditions, and there is no guarantee of success. Good Samaritan laws are designed to encourage people to give help if they can and to protect them if their best efforts fail.

George? No. George is protected by the Good Samaritan law because under the circumstances his assistance was reasonable and not reckless or negligent.

But what about the case of Ralph and Fran? They live next door to each other, with their garages separating the houses. One day while Fran is at work, Ralph returns home early. He is driving one of his company's heavy-duty trucks. As he pulls into his driveway, he sees that the shed in back of Fran's house is on fire. It has been a dry summer, and Ralph is afraid the fire will spread quickly. He doesn't have a fire extinguisher, but he knows that Fran has one in her garage. However, her garage is locked. Ralph decides to run his truck right into the garage wall to get at the extinguisher. The whole building falls down. Can Fran sue for damages even though Ralph was trying to help? Yes, she can. The courts would likely judge that Ralph was unreasonable while trying to be a Good Samaritan. He could have broken a window or forced open the door to get the extinguisher instead of knocking down the entire structure.

Three conditions must be met for a Good Samaritan to be protected under the law:

- Condition 1: The care that a Good Samaritan gives must be the result of an emergency. Suppose you hear loud noises in the next apartment and jump to the conclusion that someone is being attacked. You pick up a baseball bat, knock down your neighbor's door, and hit the first person you see. It turns out that your neighbor and some friends were dancing to loud music. There was no emergency, and you're not a Good Samaritan. In fact, you're in trouble.

- Condition 2: The person who is protected by the Good Samaritan law can't be the person who caused the emergency in the first place. In late 1998, for example, a New York doctor—seemingly a Good Samaritan—picked up an injured person from the street and brought her into a hospital emergency room. It was later found that the doctor herself had run over the injured person and did not report it! Needless to say, she won't be protected by the Good Samaritan law.

- Condition 3: Emergency care by the Good Samaritan must not be given in a reckless or negligent manner. An emergency ambulance driver is off duty and drinking heavily in a bar. On his way home he witnesses a serious auto accident. He sees a man pinned under one of the cars. In his drunken state, he forgets to be cautious and simply pulls on the victim's leg to free him. The car shifts and crushes the victim. The ambulance driver won't be protected from liability, for his conduct was reckless.

Of course, not all situations involving Good Samaritans are so obvious. Sometimes the line between appropriate action and recklessness or negligence is hard to decide. Take, for instance, the 1995 Vermont case of *Hardingham v. United Counseling Service of Bennington County*. David Hardingham, a recovering alcoholic, worked for United Counseling Service. When he didn't show up for work one day, some of his coworkers went to his apartment and found him drunk. In fact, they saw him drinking windshield wiper fluid. Although the coworkers got him to a hospital, they didn't tell the medical team what he had been drinking. As a result, Hardingham was not treated properly and lost his eyesight. He sued his company. The Vermont Supreme Court sided against him, however, saying that even though his coworkers didn't reveal that Hardingham had drunk windshield wiper fluid, they probably did save his life. The fact that they didn't tell the medical authorities what he had been drinking was not proof, said the court, that they were indifferent to him or negligent.

One of the Vermont justices, however, disagreed with the decision. He said that Hardingham's coworkers, in failing to disclose that he had been drinking windshield wiper fluid, had omitted the most important fact about his condition. The court's decision, said the dissenting justice, was rendered because no one, not even judges, wants to find a well-meaning Good Samaritan liable for coming to someone's aid.

Most states try to protect the protector by a fairly simple general doctrine such as the one Utah has on its books concerning the acts of Good Samaritans. Utah law says: "A person who renders emergency care at or near the scene of, or during an emergency, gratuitously and in good faith, is not liable for any civil damages or penalties as a result of any act or omission by the person rendering the emergency care, unless the person is grossly negligent or caused the emergency."

Although the Good Samaritan laws in all states are similar to varying degrees, there are some key differences. Many states offer immunity only to doctors, nurses, or other medical professionals. But the law in Pennsylvania, for example, protects anyone, whether a medical specialist or not, who renders aid. Included in the Pennsylvania Good Samaritan law is a "good faith" clause. It says that the person who gives aid must have a "reasonable opinion" that the aid is necessary and that it cannot wait until the victim reaches a hospital.

Note that doctors who act as Good Samaritans, meaning in part that they do not expect to be paid, are protected from liability. A doctor "at work"—that is, giving services for which he or she is to be compensated—can be sued if the patient deems the work rendered to be grossly negligent, for instance. An interesting case in Illinois, *Johnson v. Matviuw,* points out the difference. A patient in a hospital suffered cardiac arrest. The nurse called for help to a doctor who happened to be in the next room but was not the patient's physician. Despite the doctor's intervention, the patient died, and the family later sued. The doctor claimed that he had been acting as a Good Samaritan and was therefore not liable. The court agreed, saying that in this instance the doctor was providing emergency medical treatment without expectation of money. The fact that the emergency was in a hospital did not change the Good Samaritan situation.

What about doctors and other medical personnel who are in the military? Can they be sued? No. But the U.S. government can. Before 1946, the federal government could not be sued. After that, however, the Federal Tort Claims Act allowed the government to be held liable if a patient was injured in a military or other federal hospital. In 1974 the Gonzales Act established that the government can be sued for the negligence of a military doctor, nurse, or other medical personnel, but the individual medical worker cannot be held liable.

As different situations present themselves and society changes, so do Good Samaritan laws. Some states specify that the caregiver cannot expect money for the service rendered. Of course, this would not be the case in certain situations. An ambulance driver, for instance, who gave medical emergency care other than mere transportation would certainly expect to be paid. In Minnesota, Good Samaritan laws cover those who come to the aid of people injured in hazardous-material fires or explosions.

Another sign of the times can be found in Nevada's Good Samaritan statutes. People who attempt to help a heart attack victim are protected from liability if they have completed the training requirements to offer cardiopulmonary resuscitation or have been trained in the use of a defibrillator, a device that applies an electric shock to the victim's chest in order to restore the heart to a normal rhythm. You're also protected if you are part of a search-and-rescue team and under the orders of the county sheriff.

It's clear that the laws of most states are set up to encourage bystanders to come to the aid of people in trouble if they can, and to protect them from criminal or civil action if they do. And it is probably true that most people would want to help someone in danger if they could without endangering themselves, or being sued later. If we agree that Good Samaritan laws are a good thing for a moral society, what about the next step? Would it be a good thing to *insist* that a person be a Good Samaritan, to force him or her to help an individual in distress? Is it moral to charge a person with a duty to rescue? What might be the downsides of such a requirement? How does government in the United States deal with these issues? In the next chapter, we'll take a look at some of these questions.

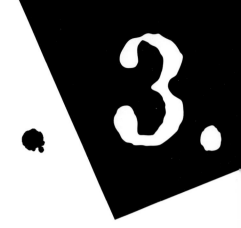

THE STATE
OF THE STATES

Rhode Island, the smallest of the 50 states, has a duty to rescue law. This is especially interesting because Rhode Island's statute is a direct result of what happened in neighboring Massachusetts, which doesn't have such a law. In the 1980s a particularly horrendous assault took place at Big Dan's Bar in New Bedford. A young woman was raped by several men while patrons watched or cheered but did nothing to stop the crime. (The case inspired a 1988 movie, *The Accused*, in which Jodie Foster starred as the victim fighting for justice, a role for which she won an Academy Award.) In real life, Massachusetts had no law at the time of the gang rape under which

A scene from the 1988 movie The Accused, *starring Jodie Foster (left) as the victim of a gang rape, and Kelly McGillis (center) as her lawyer. In the actual case that inspired the motion picture, patrons in a New Bedford, Massachusetts, bar watched and cheered as a woman was gang-raped. Under Massachusetts law, the bystanders' failure to aid the rape victim couldn't be punished.*

the bar patrons could be prosecuted for doing nothing to aid the victim. It still doesn't. But lawmakers in Rhode Island were so outraged by the incident that they passed their own law in 1987. In Rhode Island anyone witnessing a sexual assault—or a murder, manslaughter, or armed robbery—must report it, if the person can do so without peril to himself or herself. The penalty for not reporting such a crime is a fine of up to $1,000 and a possible six months in jail.

Rhode Island is one of only four U.S. states that have duty to rescue laws. The other three are Minnesota, Vermont, and Wisconsin. Other states are currently considering such legislation. Ever since the murder of little Sherrice Iverson in 1997, and the failure of bystander David Cash even to report the crime, activists in Nevada have been pushing for a duty to rescue law for their state.

Why aren't more such laws on the books? At first glance it seems obvious that the men who did nothing to aid the rape victim in that New Bedford bar should face the possibility of legal penalties. But the issue isn't quite as cut-and-dried as one might think. American legislators are wary of passing laws that could create a "slippery slope" regarding the duty to rescue. In other words, drawing the line between when a citizen should be legally obligated to help a person in trouble and when such help is not required can be quite problematic. While a law might be passed in response to the most flagrant cases, such as the New Bedford gang rape, the law might inevitably apply to a host of less clear-cut cases. The ultimate result, legislators worry, could be a society in which people are obliged to become virtual agents of the police by informing on their neighbors.

Suppose, for instance, that a law required, under penalty of a stiff fine, that all adults report any signs of physical abuse in children. Mary works in a school cafeteria. One day she notices that little Mark has a terrible bruise on his upper arm. It looks to Mary as though someone squeezed his arm very tightly. Mary doesn't know Mark, and she isn't sure that he has been abused. However, she is afraid that if she doesn't report the bruise and it turns out to have been caused by child abuse, she might be fined under the law. So Mary tells the school principal, who investigates and finds that Mark fell off a swing a few days earlier while playing with some of his friends. Though there was no abuse, Mary did what the law required. End of story? Not quite. Now Mark's mother is outraged because the word around town is that she was suspected of abusing her son. She threatens to sue the school—and Mary. Such things have happened. This makes lawmakers extremely cautious.

Legislators sometimes point to the former Soviet Union as an example of what can happen when citizens are encouraged to inform on their neighbors, whether it be through duty to rescue laws or simply through government policy. Under Communist rule in the early and mid-20th century, Soviet citizens were encouraged to report anyone who committed an offense against the state, and they were rewarded for doing so. From that starting point, citizens quite naturally began reporting not only crimes against the state, but any crimes. In time, the practice of informing became so widespread that some citizens were telling practically everything they knew about anyone. The result was near chaos and an erosion of privacy.

Yolanda Manuel, the mother of murder victim Sherrice Iverson, becomes the first person to sign a petition urging the Nevada legislature to create a duty to rescue law. The proposed law would require that witnesses report any attack on a child.

In the United States, legislators at all levels of government are wary about going down that same slippery slope. Lawmakers walk a fine line when it comes to duty to rescue laws. Let's take a look at the statutes in Minnesota, Vermont, and Wisconsin.

Minnesota Statute 604A.01, passed in 1998, is called the Good Samaritan Law. Two of its subdivisions, however, clearly distinguish between Good Samaritan acts and a duty to rescue.

The subdivision concerning Good Samaritans is called "General Immunity from Liability." It basically says that anyone who offers assistance at the scene of an emergency, without expecting to be paid, cannot be sued for the care given unless that care was applied in a reckless or wanton manner. In other words, the care need only be reasonable to protect the Good Samaritan from liability. You see a man fall out of a second-story window. He is unconscious, and from the look of it his leg is broken. Covering him with a blanket or your coat and calling the police or an ambulance is reasonable care. Attempting to set his broken leg when you don't know how is not.

The subdivision that concerns the duty to rescue in Minnesota is called "Duty to Assist." It says that a person at the scene of an emergency who sees that another person is in grave physical harm must give "reasonable" assistance to the victim. That assistance may be no more than calling authorities to obtain medical aid. However, you are not expected to give assistance under this statute if by doing so you would put yourself in harm's way. In other words, you don't have to try to save a person drowning in deep water if you can't swim. And you don't have to walk into the line of fire to rescue someone who has just been shot.

If you don't obey the duty to assist law in Minnesota, you are guilty of a misdemeanor. In the United States, criminal offenses are classified according to the seriousness of the crime and punished accordingly, although the distinctions are sometimes blurred. The most serious crimes are called felonies and are typically punishable by not less than one year in prison. Murder, for instance, is a felony; so is armed bank robbery. A misdemeanor is a lesser charge and may be punishable by only a fine, or perhaps a short stay in the local jail. Being drunk and disorderly is a misdemeanor; so is failing to pay traffic tickets or, in Minnesota, failing to assist at the scene of an emergency.

The duty to rescue law in Vermont concerns emergency medical care, under Vermont Statute 12-23-519, passed in 1997. Like Minnesota, Vermont uses the word *reasonable*. You're expected to help someone in danger if you can give reasonable assistance without putting yourself in harm's way. If you don't, you can be fined up to $100. However, the Vermont statute stipulates that if you do give reasonable assistance, you can't be sued for the consequences. Remember Jack in chapter 2, who broke Joe's ribs while trying to dislodge a chicken bone? That assistance is reasonable under Vermont law, and Jack can't be held liable for Joe's cracked ribs.

Remember that medical professionals are not protected by Good Samaritan laws *if* the treatment they give can be proven to be negligent or careless. Doctors in Vermont felt that this tended to discourage medical personnel from helping in an emergency, so they tried to get a statute passed to change that situation. But Vermont legislators didn't buy it. Doctors can be sued in Vermont if the treatment they offer is negligent or careless. The fine for violations, however, is just $100.

Vermont's so-called Good Samaritan statute ends with an interesting phrase. It says that you must give reasonable assistance in an emergency "unless that assistance or care is being provided by others." That might lead to a curious predicament.

Here's one possible scenario. Jake is having dinner in a local bar and grill with his girlfriend. Nearby is a table of six young men who look and act like the town

tough guys. They are also having dinner and have obviously had a little too much to drink. Suddenly, one of them starts to choke on whatever he is eating. After a few moments, one of his friends jumps up and hits him on the back, but that doesn't work. Soon all the young men are crowded around the victim. As the minutes go by, one of the young men yells for a doctor.

Jake is not a doctor, but he has taken a course for this medical emergency. Nevertheless, he is wary about getting involved with this group. What if he doesn't do it right? Will they turn on him? So Jake does nothing, hoping that one of the victim's friends will successfully dislodge the object.

Finally, one of the victim's friends, now in a panic, yells again for help. Jake, who now sees that the choker is turning blue around the lips, runs over, gets behind the victim, and performs the Heimlich maneuver to dislodge the piece of bone the man had swallowed. The victim lives, but the extended time he went without oxygen has caused brain damage.

Jake has saved the young man's life with his treatment, but if he had acted earlier, he could probably have prevented the brain damage. Can Jake be sued, or is he protected by the phrase in the Vermont statute, "unless that assistance or care is being provided by others"? It's an interesting question.

Wisconsin's duty to rescue law, passed in 1995 as Statute 940.34, comes under the heading of "duty to aid victim or report crime." As in the other states, you're guilty of a misdemeanor in Wisconsin if you know that a crime is being committed and a person is being exposed to bodily harm, but you don't offer "reasonable" help or call the police. You're also guilty of a misdemeanor in Wisconsin if you are licensed as a private detective and you don't notify police when you have reasonable grounds to think that a crime is being committed.

As in the other states, Wisconsin protects its Good Samaritan citizens. You need not obey the duty to rescue law in the Badger State if by doing so you would put yourself in danger or neglect your duty to another person. For instance, if you were walking an infant in a stroller, you would not be expected to leave the child alone while you ran down the street to help someone who had just been hurt. But you might try to get to a phone to call for help as soon as possible. Wisconsin also offers immunity from prosecution for the Good Samaritan.

Although "duty to rescue" is the law to some degree in only 4 of the 50 states, by custom we expect and want people to behave a certain way during emergencies, even if they are not legally required to do so. Courts have found, however, that in certain situations a special relationship exists that overrides the general rule that there is no duty to rescue. That special relationship of itself creates a duty to rescue. The most obvious such relationship is between parent and child. It is accepted that a parent has a duty to assist his or her child in danger. However, customary law recognizes other special relationships that don't, at first glance, seem so obvious. Let's look at some important cases that involve what the courts saw as special relationships that created a duty to rescue.

Is there a special relationship between an officer of the law and a bystander? In the state of Virginia, there is. An innocent bystander saw one motorist beating another after an accident. When the bystander intervened, he was himself beaten with a shovel and a pipe. Along came a deputy sheriff, in uniform and on duty. The sheriff watched but did nothing to stop the assault. In *Burdette v. Marks*, the Virginia Supreme Court ruled against the sheriff in 1992. The court said that a special relationship exists between someone in peril and an on-duty officer of the law. In other words, the sheriff had a legal duty to aid the victim.

Is there a special relationship between friends? After *Farwell v. Keaton* in 1966, Michigan said yes, under certain circumstances. Two friends, Siegrist and Farwell, were chased by a gang one evening. Siegrist got away, but Farwell was badly beaten. However, he managed to return to his car, where Siegrist found him and put ice on his severe head wound. For the next couple of hours, while Farwell slept in the backseat, his friend drove around town. Finally, Siegrist parked the car in the driveway of Farwell's grandparents' home. Unable to wake his friend, Siegrist left him in the backseat of the car and went home. Farwell's grandparents found him the next morning and took him to the hospital, but it was too late. He died of his injuries three days later. His family sued Siegrist and the gang members (one of them was Keaton, named in the suit).

The Michigan Supreme Court ruled against Siegrist, finding that a special relationship exists between two people on a social outing. On such an occasion, according to the court, it is implied that one friend will help another in danger. Knowing that his friend was badly hurt, Siegrist was negligent in leaving him alone in the car. If Siegrist had been unaware that Farwell was seriously injured, however, the court would not have ruled against him. Also, the court pointed out, Siegrist could have gotten medical aid without endangering himself.

How about psychotherapists? Do they have a duty to rescue? The state supreme court of California thought so in the 1976 case of *Tarasoff v. University of California*. A man named Prosenjit Poddar informed his psychotherapist, Dr. Lawrence Moore, that he was going to kill Tariana Tarasoff. Though he believed Poddar's threat, Moore was told by his own psychiatric chief that he could not warn the woman. Poddar did, in fact, murder Tarasoff, and her family sued the University of California, which ran the psychiatric service.

A lower court dismissed the case, ruling that there was no law in California compelling a person to rescue a stranger. Therefore, Moore had no duty to warn Tarasoff. The California Supreme Court agreed that there was no duty to rescue law, but it nevertheless reversed the decision and ruled for Tarasoff's family. It said that under certain circumstances, if a therapist believes his or her patient poses grave harm to another, the therapist has a duty to warn the intended victim.

Do employees and employers have a special relationship? That has been commonly recognized as far back as 1945, in the case of *Szabo v. Pennsylvania RR*.

In general, Americans have no obligation under the law to assist someone in an emergency. But various courts have identified certain exceptions, when there is a "special relationship" between the people involved. Such a relationship exists, the Michigan Supreme Court found in a 1966 case, when friends are on an outing together.

After working in the hot sun all day, a railroad worker suffered heat stroke. His coworkers were told to take him home, which they did. But there they left him alone, and because he received no medical care, he died. The Pennsylvania court hearing the case said that the employer—the railroad—had a duty to give the employee reasonable medical assistance. The railroad as employer had also been held liable in Mississippi years earlier, in the case of *Yazoo, MS. Railway v. Byrd*. This time a passenger, through no fault of the railway, fell off a train. Instead of coming to his aid, rail workers just left him on the tracks, and he died. The court found against the railway for not offering assistance to its passenger.

From these examples, we can see that under special circumstances, state courts do imply that there is a duty to rescue. But what happens if you actually try to stop a rescue or interfere with someone else's rescue attempt? In 1983 the case of *Soldano v. O'Daniels* concerned just that question. A Good Samaritan came upon a man being attacked on the sidewalk. He ran across the street and asked the store employee to call the police. The worker refused. Then the Good Samaritan asked for the phone so he could call the police himself. The worker again refused. The California court held the owner of the business liable for his employee's refusal to help the Good Samaritan. The court said that the owner of land that is open to the public—in this case the business owner—has a duty, if not to give assistance, then at least not to interfere with someone else's rescue attempt.

It's not always easy to see where responsibility or morality lies when the subject of the duty to rescue comes up. Some cases may seem quite obvious, but as we know, these issues aren't always as simple as they seem or so easy to judge. Laws mandating a duty to rescue have many critics. Some people agree with John Stuart Mill that such laws infringe on personal liberty.

Some argue that morality can't be legislated. Others feel that creating a duty to rescue opens too big a can of worms regarding people's actions. Still others say that such a duty would be impossible to enforce. Perhaps this slippery slope is the main reason that the U.S. Congress has never passed a federal law mandating a duty to rescue.

Not that Congress hasn't tried. One of the latest attempts, in the 1990s, was a House of Representatives bill concerning "duties for aiding injured persons." As background the proposed bill pointed out that duty to rescue statutes are operational in several European countries, that four U.S. states have some duty to rescue provisions on the books, and that other states stipulate certain instances when a special relationship exists, such as a parent's duty to rescue a child. The House bill proposed the establishment of a duty to rescue statute, violation of which would be punishable by 90 days in jail, a $1,000 fine, or both. Most legislators, however, never believed the bill had a chance to pass, and it never got to the House floor for a vote.

American legislators for the most part are reluctant to impose duty to rescue restrictions on citizens. That is much less true, however, of lawmakers in the rest of the world.

THE STATE
OF OTHER
COUNTRIES

Avenue of the Righteous Gentiles, Jerusalem. In front of each tree is a plaque with the name and country of a person who risked his or her life to save Jews from persecution by the Nazis during World War II.

Suppose a man sees a three-year-old merrily chasing a butterfly across a field and heading right for an uncovered, abandoned mine shaft. Without endangering himself in the slightest, the man could block the child's path and save her from grave injury or possible death. But he does nothing. The child trots on, falls into the shaft, and is killed.

One might argue that the man has no morals, but under American law he has done nothing illegal. Therefore, he cannot be prosecuted for the child's death.

Many countries in the rest of the world, however, take a different approach. For instance, although European nations generally operate under codes not very different on most issues from British and American law (which are closely related), they do regard the duty to rescue in a different light. Beginning with Portugal in 1867, some European nations have specifically charged their citizens with a duty to rescue. This goes beyond,

45

for example, a law (also enforced in the United States) against leaving the scene of an accident that a driver caused or was involved in. But that law punishes some-one for doing something—running away—not for doing nothing. And it doesn't pertain to innocent bystanders.

Shortly after Portugal first imposed a duty to rescue, Germany adopted its Criminal Code of 1870. It said that a German citizen must obey a police command to give aid in the case of an accident or common danger. When Adolf Hitler and the Nazi Party took control of Germany in the 1930s, the code was expanded. Police could demand aid from citizens for much more than just an accident or common danger. Failure to obey resulted in high fines and up to two years in jail. After World War II, the supreme court of what was then West Germany took a look at the supposed harshness of this duty to rescue code. The court decided that there had always been a "moral obligation" to help one's neighbor and that enforcing that obligation had not been the invention of the Nazis. The law remained, with slight changes. Since 1953 the German duty to rescue law has read: "Whoever does not render help in case of accident, common danger or necessity although help is required and under the circumstances is exactable, and in particular is possible without danger of serious injury to himself and without violation of other important duties, will be punished by imprisonment up to one year or by fine."

Two former European Communist countries wanted Good Samaritan behavior and the duty to rescue to be part of their political agendas. But the Soviet Union and Czechoslovakia handled the attempt in different ways. In the Soviet Union, which split into a dozen independent republics in 1991, Article 130 of the Constitution of 1936 said that all citizens had an affirmative duty with respect to the laws of "socialist intercourse." Being a Good Samaritan was quickly defined as one of

Under the Nazi regime of Adolf Hitler (shown here), German citizens had a legal duty to give aid if so ordered by a police officer. Failure to comply resulted in stiff fines and up to two years' imprisonment.

those laws. Two years later a Russian scholar suggested that Article 130 made it legally binding for a Russian citizen to aid another. Following that, in 1948 a statute was proposed that would require citizens, under threat of penalty, to intervene personally if necessary to protect another person's life or property, or at least to notify authorities. However, the statute was never enacted as part of the Soviet constitution, which is perhaps surprising because this Communist country tolerated many more restrictions on personal freedoms than do democratic nations such as the United States.

Soviet legal scholars, however, seemed to feel that one's duty to rescue was a common law recognized by all and therefore did not need to be codified.

Such was not the case in Czechoslovakia (which in 1993 became two separate states, the Czech Republic and Slovakia). In 1964, the Czechoslovak Civil Code made it a citizen's duty to prevent "injury to health and damage to property or undue enrichment to the detriment of society or individuals." This was an obvious effort to foster Good Samaritan behavior. The Czechoslovak citizen had two specific duties: to notify appropriate authorities immediately in case of emergency or danger, and to intervene personally in the emergency if he or she could do so without personal harm. A citizen who failed to comply could be made to compensate the victim for whatever damage was determined to have occurred.

Both the Soviet Union and Czechoslovakia wanted the same thing—to encourage citizens to become Good Samaritans. However, Czechoslovakia went further than the USSR, attempting to enforce Communist morality through the law.

Unlike much of Europe, Great Britain has no duty to rescue laws and no Good Samaritan laws. The closest the British come is their Road and Traffic Act. In England you are guilty of an offense if you do not report a traffic accident.

The French go a bit further. If you see a traffic accident, you must stop, call the police, and then wait for official help to arrive. In France, where such laws were influenced by the German occupation during World War II, you can not only go to jail but also be sued for refusing aid to an accident victim. In one such case, a Frenchman who apparently was not too fond of his son-in-law just walked away when the young man fell through ice. The victim managed to get out of the icy water and later successfully sued his father-in-law. The older man also went to jail for three years.

Much of western Europe has similar laws about the duty to rescue. You can be fined and go to prison for three months in the Netherlands if you refuse aid to someone in danger of death, especially if that person dies. The same is more or less true in Norway, Poland, Italy, and Turkey.

Denmark's duty to rescue doctrine took on a unique aspect during the early years of World War II. The head bishop of the Danish Lutheran Church received a secret message from a Danish agent working in Germany. The message warned of grave trouble coming to Danish Jews. This was, of course, the beginning of the Holocaust, the Nazi drive to rid the world of all Jews, as well as other so-called undesirables. On behalf of the church, the bishop issued a decree stipulating that Danish Lutherans must help the Jews. The decree was treated as though it were law. After the Germans occupied Denmark, numerous Danes hid their Jewish neighbors and friends or got them to Sweden or to other safe countries. Whereas the Nazis decimated Jewish populations throughout Europe, some 95 percent of Denmark's Jews survived the Holocaust. To honor those who had helped save Jews during the Nazi persecution, Israelis later created a tree-lined walkway in Jerusalem known as the Avenue of the Righteous Gentiles.

Concerning the innocent bystander and a duty to rescue, the Jewish legal system has historically been influenced by the Code of Maimonides (1135–1204). It states: "If one person is able to save another and does not save him, he transgresses the commandment, *Neither shalt thou stand idly by the blood of thy neighbor* (Leviticus 19:16). Similarly, if one person sees another drowning in the sea, or being attacked by bandits, or being attacked by wild animals, and although able to rescue him either alone or by hiring others, does not rescue him . . . he transgresses."

The code takes failure to aid a neighbor very seriously, saying: "[T]he offense is most serious, for if one

Copies of the Torah, which contains the body of Jewish law. The Jewish tradition has always strongly encouraged bystanders to come to the aid of people in trouble. But, Jewish scholars say, a rescuer need not endanger his or her life to save another.

destroys the life of a single Israelite, it is regarded as though he destroyed the whole world, and if one preserves the life of a single Israelite, it is regarded as though he preserved the whole world (Maimonides Torts, "Murder and Preservation of Life" 1:14). Such a statement has been interpreted by Jewish scholars in various ways. Most take the Code of Maimonides literally, saying that "thou shalt not rise against the blood of thy neighbor" means that one must not threaten a neighbor's life by speech or deed. Some say it means that one must not give false or slanderous testimony against a neighbor in court. Still others interpret the words as meaning that one should not stand idly by when a neighbor is in danger.

Modern lawyers in Israel refer to a centuries-old verse quoted by masters of the Talmud, the authoritative body of Jewish law, as the "law of the Good Samaritan." If a bystander is encouraged to rescue someone in danger, what if the rescue would put the bystander's own life in danger? Does that make self-sacrifice a legal duty according to Talmudic law? No, say modern scholars. A person need not give up his own life to save the life of someone else.

Jewish law, which encourages the bystander to come to the aid of someone in distress, is therefore similar to the law of most European countries and differs from the law in the United Kingdom and the United States. The essential point in the Jewish law of the Good Samaritan is that one has a duty to rescue another person in distress *if* that can be done without endangering the rescuer's life.

It might seem at first glance that European and Anglo-American laws differ greatly on the subject of the duty to rescue and being a Good Samaritan. And, indeed, we see that there are differences. In practice, however, both sets of laws want the same thing: to encourage citizens to aid their neighbors if possible and without danger to themselves. In most cases under Anglo-American law, no penalty is imposed for not doing so. On the European side, however, the citizen is subject to penalties. However, victims who sue others in Europe for not being a Good Samaritan don't usually receive compensation. And in practice, criminal prosecution for not being a Good Samaritan is relatively rare, and when it does occur, the criminal penalties are usually minor.

ON THE WATER AND IN THE AIR

T he law of the sea has been, by tradition, separate in many ways from the law under which governments operate. In an interesting case from 1931, maritime law was the issue in a lawsuit.

The man who brought the suit, in *Warschauer v. Lloyd Sabaudo S.A.*, was a U.S. citizen and resident of New York City. One day in October, Warschauer and a companion were out for an ocean cruise when their motorboat engine died. With no fuel, food, or means of communication, they were in real trouble when they saw the Italian steamship *Conte Biancamano* within hailing distance. Although the ship's crew saw their distress signals, the steamship didn't stop but instead sailed on into port. Warschauer and his friend were saved by the U.S. Coast Guard two days later. He later sued the Italian company that owned the ship for not coming to their aid.

The court ruled against Warschauer. Why? Because it was the captain of the ship, not the owner, who failed

A Coast Guard helicopter departs for a ship rescue off the coast of New Jersey. While the Coast Guard coordinates rescues in U.S. coastal waters, by tradition anyone who encounters someone in trouble on the seas is supposed to offer assistance if possible.

to give aid. Should the owner—the employer—have been liable for the actions of his employee, the ship's captain? According to the 1910 International Salvage Treaty, drafted by some 20 nations, including the United States, the answer is no. Article 11 of the treaty says that every ship's captain "is bound, so far as he can do so without serious danger to his vessel, her crew and passengers, to render assistance to everybody, even though an enemy, found at sea in danger of being lost." It also says that the owner of the vessel is not responsible if the ship's captain does not honor that obligation.

Another interesting case involving danger on the water took place in the early years of the century on an island in Lake Champlain, between New York and Vermont. A man, woman, and their two small children were sailing on the lake when a violent storm came up. Thinking that their boat was in danger, they sailed to a dock and tied up. The owner of the dock, and also of the whole island, was apparently not the friendly sort. He untied the boat. It drifted out in the storm, was driven back, and crashed into the shore, destroying the boat and injuring the passengers.

The owner of the boat sued. The defendant argued that the boat owner had trespassed upon his land and that he had every right to evict trespassers. However, in deciding the case, called *Ploff v. Putnam,* the Vermont court stated a "doctrine of necessity." It said in effect that the boat owner had no choice but to trespass in this instance because he was in danger of having himself and his family carried away in the storm. Under such circumstances, the court declared, trespassing upon another's property is justified.

An even stranger case concerning the doctrine of necessity had occurred much earlier in England. A ferryman was taking 47 passengers, including a dead man in a coffin, on his barge for a trip to London. When a storm blew up on the river, the barge appeared to be in danger of going down. The ferryman decided that the only way to save the barge was to throw out something heavy. That turned out to be the casket—which, of course, contained the body. The dead man's family sued.

In finding for the ferryman, the court ruled that the doctrine of necessity justified losing the dead body and casket to save the lives of others. Not many rescue problems on the water present such an unusual situation.

There are actually no duty to rescue laws at sea, according to Chief Petty Officer Robert Linier of the U.S. Coast Guard. There are no Good Samaritan sea laws either. However, says Linier, it is assumed that you will help another person in peril on the water if you can. In addition, certain organizations have been formed for the purpose of sea rescues. One of them is called AMVER.

AMVER, which stands for Automatic Maritime Vessel Response, is an emergency organization of merchant vessels that are equipped to perform at-sea rescues. All activities are coordinated through a Coast Guard center in Washington, D.C. Once an emergency signal is received from any type of boat or ship on the ocean, a merchant vessel responds to offer assistance until a Coast Guard cutter or helicopter can reach the area.

Although there are no duty to rescue laws at sea, a U.S. federal code dictates that anyone who witnesses a boating accident or is involved in one must report it. As a witness, you need only call the authorities. If you are personally involved, you must report the details of the mishap in writing. This applies only if there is damage to the vessel or vessels or they are lost—or, of course, if a person is injured in the accident, dies, or disappears at sea. According to federal boating law, injury, death, or disappearance must be reported within 45 hours; property loss, within 10 days.

Whenever there is talk of trouble at sea, most people probably think of the doomed ship *Titanic*, which struck an iceberg and sank in the icy waters of the

This page: The stricken luxury liner Andrea Doria, *listing badly after a mid-ocean collision with another ship, July 26, 1956. Facing page: Sailors move an injured passenger. The loss of life from the* Andrea Doria *accident was relatively small, thanks in large part to the actions of Good Samaritans aboard the ship and to the quick response of rescue vessels.*

North Atlantic on the night of April 14, 1912. The great luxury liner took more than 1,500 passengers and crew to a watery grave; 705 were rescued. (That dramatic story was made into three movies: the 1953 British film *A Night to Remember* and two American films called *Titanic*, one released in 1953, and the other—the winner of 11 Academy Awards—released in 1997.) Terrible as the *Titanic* disaster was, a later event led to what has been called the greatest sea rescue in modern history. It gave quite a few people—professional and otherwise—an unexpected, and surely undesired, opportunity to earn the title of Good Samaritan.

Late in the evening of July 25, 1956, the beautiful Italian luxury liner *Andrea Doria* was on the last leg of its journey to New York City, having left Genoa, Italy,

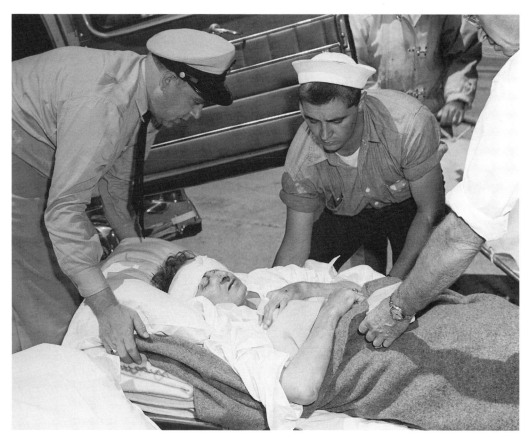

on July 17. On this, the ship's 101st crossing, probably no one on board except for the captain—who was by nature a cautious man—gave a thought to disaster. Why should they? Every safety feature learned over hundreds of years of shipbuilding, and from countless maritime accidents, had been incorporated into the three-year-old pride of the Italian merchant fleet. One of the simplest, yet most significant, safety features had resulted from the *Titanic* disaster. The *Titanic* had not carried sufficient lifeboat capacity: with more than 2,200 passengers and crew on board, the ship had room in her lifeboats for only 1,178 persons. This was the primary reason for the huge loss of life. The *Andrea Doria*, in contrast, carried 1,706 passengers and crew but had lifeboat seating capacity for 2,000.

The *Titanic* had been called unsinkable. The *Andrea Doria*, it was thought, really was. However, in the dense fog off Nantucket Island in the northern Atlantic, the Swedish liner *Stockholm*, built to withstand icebergs in Scandinavia, crashed into the side of the *Andrea Doria*.

Throughout that night and dark morning, people reacted to the disaster in various ways. Some of the liner's crew risked death as they struggled for hours to free passengers from the twisted steel and guide them into lifeboats. Other crew members jumped into the lifeboats ahead of the passengers they had promised to protect. Some passengers lost their own lives trying to help others. Some stole life jackets from the wounded to save themselves. In all, only 51 lives were lost, a testimony to those who played the Good Samaritan role to its fullest.

Shortly after 10:10 on the morning of July 26, passengers and crew stared in awe and disbelief from the ships that had converged on the area to rescue survivors of the accident. The deadly fog had lifted, so all could watch the death of the great liner as it slowly disappeared. It came to rest 225 feet beneath the surface of the Atlantic Ocean. It is still there.

An inquiry ruled that the captains of both ships were at fault for the collision in the fog. The *Andrea Doria*'s captain, Piero Calamai, retired to his home in Genoa afterward. It is said that he never once talked about the disaster, but as he lay dying in 1972, he called out to his daughter, "Are the passengers saved?"

Do the rules of law or common sense concerning rescue on the ocean apply to rescue in the air? Are people expected to respond differently if they are above the land or water? Actually, no. The same expectations and protections exist no matter what is beneath your feet. "What's law on the ground," it is said, "is law in the air." A Good Samaritan who would assist someone on the ground can expect to assist someone in the air without fear of prosecution if the assistance is reasonable and sensible. Indeed, there have been many instances of passengers or crew members aiding those who became ill during a flight.

But the ability of Good Samaritans, especially doctors, to help a stricken passenger is often limited by a lack of medical equipment on hand. In the event of cardiac arrest, for example, a defibrillator is often necessary. But airplanes don't typically carry these devices. That may soon change, however. In 1998, a lawsuit was brought against the German airline Lufthansa by the family of a man who suffered a fatal heart attack during a flight. The suit charged that the airline was negligent in obtaining medical treatment for the victim because the plane was not diverted to the nearest airport. The flight was diverted from its original schedule, but the suit contends that the delay caused the victim's death. The case is still pending.

To forestall such lawsuits in the future, the airlines are considering putting defibrillators and perhaps other medical devices on planes. Flight attendants must, of course, be trained in their use. But some airlines fear a move in this direction might only bring on more lawsuits.

The call for defibrillators and other medical devices was encouraged by the Aero Space Medical Association. This professional group is concerned with safety and medical improvements in the air and in space. Although not connected with the government, the worldwide association is made up of astronauts, members of the National Aeronautics and Space Administration (NASA), research scientists, and physicians.

Doctors in private practice also applaud the idea of planes carrying medical devices to help any Good Samaritan physician in the air. More than once doctors have stated that they would have gladly given medical assistance during a flight had the necessary equipment been on board.

Jubilant Israelis celebrate the success of the Entebbe hostage-rescue mission. The 1976 incident, which began when Palestinian terrorists hijacked a French airliner to Uganda, provided dramatic examples not only of military prowess but also of Good Samaritan behavior: the Air France crew defied the terrorists and insisted upon remaining with the Jewish hostages.

In 1976 a different sort of air emergency led to a celebrated rescue—and to a lesser-known Good Samaritan story. On June 27 Palestinian terrorists hijacked an Air France jetliner en route from Israel to France after its stop in Athens, Greece. The hijackers ordered the pilots to land at Entebbe Airport in the African nation of Uganda, which was then ruled by the dictator Idi Amin. Amin was sympathetic to the Palestinians' cause and even offered Ugandan troops to assist the terrorists. At Entebbe the terrorists separated the more than 100 passengers they believed to be from Israel and released the remaining non-Jewish passengers, along with the Air France crew. In return for the safe release of their hostages, the hijackers demanded the release of 53 fellow terrorists held in prison in a number of countries, including Israel.

Why is this a Good Samaritan story? Because the crew of the Air France jetliner simply refused to be released. To the surprise of their captors, the French crew said they had a moral, if not a legal, duty to remain to help the hostages. No amount of threats could induce them to leave Entebbe.

As the rest of the world waited for the next move, Israel acted. On the night of July 3, four military transport planes carrying about 200 Israeli soldiers flew some 2,500 miles from Israel to Uganda and landed without lights on a plain near Entebbe. Moving quickly to the airport terminal, where the hostages were being held, the Israeli soldiers engaged the terrorists and their Ugandan allies in a fierce firefight. Within an hour of their landing, the Israelis had rescued the hostages and Air France crew, losing one Israeli soldier and three hostages in the process. Seven terrorists and as many as 20 Ugandan soldiers were also killed.

While hostage rescues by a nation's armed forces are a rarity, and while they don't exactly qualify as Good Samaritan behavior, civilian rescue groups have been organized to perform Good Samaritan works in a more conventional manner. The next chapter examines some of these groups.

RESCUE GROUPS: HOW FAR SHOULD THEY GO?

The United States has never had a duty to rescue law as part of its federal criminal code. But from the country's earliest days, strong ideas existed regarding how people *should* behave during an emergency. And at various times in the nation's history, private citizens have formed groups to provide protective, rescue, and even law enforcement functions, usually when it appears that the authorities can't adequately do the job.

In the early days of the Old West, for instance, there existed a marked shortage of lawmen. Most towns were lucky if they had one sheriff and perhaps a deputy or two to keep the peace. In the countryside there was even less of a law enforcement presence, with each marshal

Guardian Angels on patrol in New York City's Times Square. Founded in 1979 to help keep New York's streets and subways safe and to aid people in distress, the Guardian Angels have since expanded their membership to chapters in several U.S. states and in Europe.

typically policing a vast territory. The result was that official law enforcement simply could not be expected to respond promptly and effectively to emergencies.

To fill the gaps, private citizens joined with law enforcement officials when a crisis arose. If a gang of outlaws robbed the town bank, for example, the sheriff would organize a posse composed of himself and male residents of the town. The posse would ride after the outlaws. If it caught them, the posse was supposed to bring the lawbreakers back to face trial. But that didn't always happen. Just as there was a dearth of peace officers in the Old West, there was also a dearth of judges, and the nearest one could be hundreds of miles away. Consequently, the temptation always existed for a posse to take the law into its own hands, typically by hanging the suspected lawbreakers from the nearest tree.

In some cases groups of private citizens took this disturbing trend even further, dispensing justice—or what they considered justice—totally independently of an officer of the law. Such groups were called vigilance committees, and they frequently did their work under cover of darkness and with their faces concealed by masks. In the name of protecting their communities and seeing that justice was done, vigilantes (as members of these groups were called) sometimes broke into jails and lynched the suspects who were awaiting trial there.

Today groups devoted to community protection still exist in the United States, but in the most crucial respect they differ from the vigilance committees of the Old West: they work within the law and with police and other government organizations. Their goal is to make life better for the citizens of their own communities, to be Good Samaritans by working legally to protect and aid people. Perhaps the best known of these community rescue groups, also called crisis response groups, is the Guardian Angels.

The mission of the Guardian Angels, a group founded in 1979 by Curtis Sliwa, now a New York radio talk show host, is to develop role models in the community through volunteer safety patrols and education. The Guardian Angels are probably best known, however, for their safety patrols. What started out in New York City as the Magnificent Thirteen Subway Patrol has grown to hundreds of members. Wearing their easily recognizable red berets and T-shirts, unarmed young men and women ride the city's subways between 8 P.M. and 4 A.M. They pick the poorest, toughest neighborhoods and the most poorly lit stations. Their mission is to keep the peace. Although their largest membership is in New York City, Guardian Angel groups operate in California, Colorado, and Nevada, as well as in European countries. They are there to help, to be the Good Samaritans when they can. They carry packages for the elderly or infirm, break up fights, help lost or ill people on the subways, clean up miles of city streets, and keep the police informed of illegal or suspicious activities. In short, the Guardian Angels might be thought of as Super Good Samaritans, taking the old parable about helping one's neighbor to the fullest.

Guardian Angels can, and at times do, make citizen's arrests. But that doesn't make them any different from anyone else in the United States. Any American citizen has the power, under the law, to make an arrest if he or she views a crime in progress. Obviously, a person making a citizen's arrest could be putting himself or herself in grave danger. For most people who see a crime in progress, by far the best response is to call for help.

Although the Guardian Angels work with police, no special laws protect them. The same Good Samaritan laws that cover any citizen apply. It goes without saying, however, that the Guardian Angels are better organized and perhaps more dedicated than most.

In an effort to reach teenagers and involve them in solving problems of violence, crime, and drugs in the schools, the Guardian Angels have formed Junior Angels clubs. These members are under 16 years of age and do not participate in safety patrols on the streets.

Other organizations are dedicated to being Good Samaritans in less obvious ways. For example, Safety, Inc., founded by Carl-David Birman and also known as People for Peace, is a network of men and women dedicated to ending violence in New York City. Members work to encourage survivors of child abuse, domestic violence, and sexual assault to tell their stories through artwork; to help all people in the city solve problems without drugs or violence; to promote tolerance among the city's many diverse peoples; and to keep the public informed about how peaceful living can enrich their lives. The group's best-known project is called *Clothesline*, a display of T-shirts decorated by survivors of abuse. *Clothesline* has been displayed at the United Nations as well as various buildings in New York City and Washington, D.C.

Another hardworking Good Samaritan group is Amnesty International. Since its founding in 1961, the organization has helped more than 40,000 people around the world. Amnesty's programs are dedicated to aiding the quarter or more of the world's people who, the organization claims, are subject to violations of human rights.

This people-rescue organization came about in a unique way. In 1948, in the wake of the horrors of World War II and the Holocaust, the United Nations adopted the Universal Declaration of Human Rights. The declaration was designed to guarantee that basic human rights would be respected everywhere. In 1960, however, Portugal, which had signed the Universal Declaration of Human Rights 12 years earlier, decided that its citizens could no longer speak in opposition to official government policy. Shortly thereafter, two students toasted their graduation in a Lisbon café by raising their glasses and saying aloud, "To Liberty!" They were sent to prison.

When he heard the story of the Portuguese students,

Peter Benenson, a young lawyer in London, was furious. So began his one-year campaign to bring worldwide attention to unlawful imprisonment. The campaign was successful and led to the creation of Amnesty International.

Other groups also concentrate on specific issues to aid others. One of these is the well-known Mothers Against Drunk Driving (MADD). This victim's assistance group was started in Sacramento, California, in May 1980. Now headquartered in Dallas, Texas, MADD has many chapters around the country. Focusing on the need to be responsible when driving a car, it promotes awareness of the dangers of drunk driving and has lobbied—quite successfully over the years—for legal changes and for deterrents to driving behavior that kills.

In addition to rescue groups such as the Guardian Angels or awareness-promotion groups such as MADD, well-known individuals have through the years become models for the Good Samaritan role. One such person was Baseball Hall of Famer Roberto Clemente, who spent 17 years with the Pittsburgh Pirates. An outfielder, he won the National League batting championship four times, was its Most Valuable Player once, and became only the 11th player in the history of the major leagues to collect 3,000 hits. Tragically, Clemente's life was cut short at the age of 38. He died being a Good Samaritan.

When a devastating earthquake hit the Central American country of Nicaragua, Clemente was at home in his native Puerto Rico during the off-season. Organizing a relief drive, he managed to fill an old DC-7 cargo plane with supplies. It was scheduled to fly to the Nicaraguan capital of Managua on December 31, 1972. However, Clemente heard that the country's dictator, Anastasio Somoza, was likely to steal some of the donations for his army. Against his family's wishes,

British lawyer Peter Benenson, founder of Amnesty International.

On three separate occasions actor Tom Cruise, shown here with his wife, Nicole Kidman, has played the real-life role of Good Samaritan.

Clemente decided to go along on the flight, figuring that his fame would prevent Somoza from daring to steal the supplies.

Unfortunately, the supplies never reached Nicaragua. More tragically, neither did Roberto Clemente. Sometime after takeoff, the pilot reported that they were returning to Puerto Rico because of engine trouble. The plane, crew, and Clemente, on his Good Samaritan trip, disappeared at sea. A search by the Coast Guard found nothing.

More recently, and with a happier outcome, actor Tom Cruise has made headlines as a Good Samaritan— not once, but three times. In fact, this screen star might be billed as a one-man Good Samaritan advertisement! A few years ago Cruise and his family were vacationing on the Italian Riviera. While out on a motorboat, Cruise noticed another boat nearby that seemed to be in trouble. When its occupants got dumped overboard, without hesitation Cruise, who is a good swimmer, jumped into the water and saved them. That incident was followed by a trip to India, where Cruise attended the movie opening of *Mission: Impossible*. In the huge crowd pushing to get into the theater—and to catch a glimpse of the star—the actor noticed two young boys who seemed to be in danger of being crushed against a wall. He made his way over to the wall and lifted them to safety. In 1996 Cruise got his third chance to be a Good Samaritan. While driving home from dinner in Santa Monica, California, he saw a woman lying in the street. She was the victim of a hit-and-run driver. Cruise immediately called for help on his cellular phone, waited until the paramedics arrived, and then drove to the hospital to see that the woman was going to be okay.

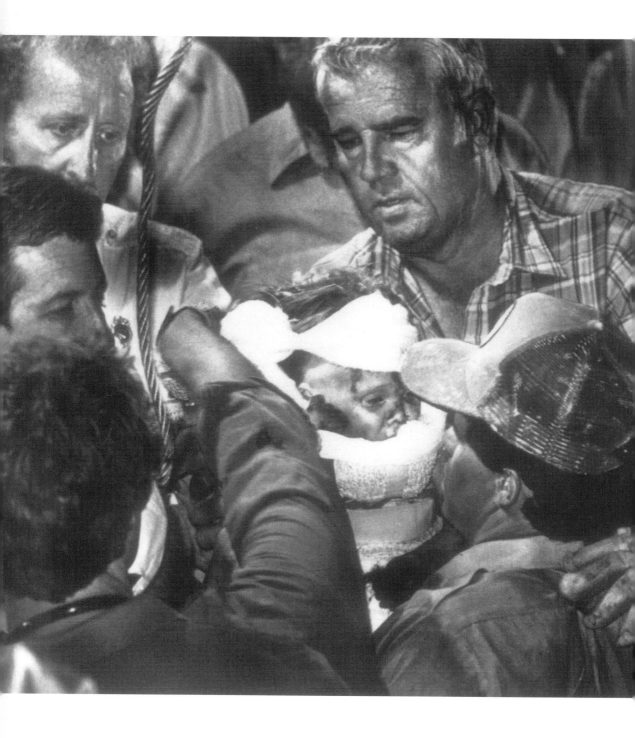

WHOSE BUSINESS IS IT ANYWAY?

Have you ever wondered what you would do if an emergency took place and you were called on to do something? Most people probably have wondered about that at one time or another. But some people actually spend their lives waiting for emergencies to happen. They are the professionals, the people for whom being a Good Samaritan represents a career.

One professional Good Samaritan story that held American TV viewers spellbound took place in 1987, when Jessica McClure, an 18-month-old toddler in Midland, Texas, toppled down an uncovered well. Her

After a frantic, 58-hour effort, rescuers succeeded in freeing 18-month-old Jessica McClure from the narrow well shaft into which she had fallen. The dramatic rescue, which took place in Midland, Texas, in 1987, involved dozens of volunteers as well as professional firefighters and emergency personnel. Tragically, the firefighter who tunneled to the shaft where Baby Jessica was trapped and pulled her out later committed suicide.

frantic mother called the Midland Fire Department. The plight of the child who quickly became known as "Baby Jessica" soon became a nationwide concern. When fireman Robert O'Donnell arrived, he quickly realized that he was confronting an almost impossible rescue problem. The well shaft was only 8 to 14 inches wide, far too narrow for an adult to go down to rescue the toddler. And Baby Jessica was too young to climb a rope lowered into the well.

How could they reach the child? How long could she survive in that dark hole without food or water? After assessing the situation and finding their options limited, the rescuers made a decision: they would drill another shaft parallel to the well, an operation that would take many hours. When it was completed, Jessica's family and a nationwide TV audience held its breath as O'Donnell was lowered 22 feet down into the dark hole. When he reached bottom, he tunneled over to the well shaft.

At last O'Donnell gave the signal to pull him up. To everyone's great relief, the fireman emerged holding a very grimy, frightened, but alive little girl. The entire operation had taken 58 hours.

Eight years later a note of sadness marred the happy ending for Baby Jessica and her family. O'Donnell, then 38, committed suicide. It was said that the success of the rescue was offset by all the other deaths he had witnessed during his 11-year career.

Every so often an incident of such horror occurs that paid professionals and ordinary citizens alike are shocked into thinking hard about Good Samaritan issues. Little Sherrice Iverson was murdered in 1997, and we asked why bystander David Cash didn't even report the crime, let alone try to stop it. That same year Princess Diana of England was killed in a car crash, and people wondered why the photographers chasing her car didn't come to her aid. Even a popular TV sitcom, *Seinfeld*, got into the act with its last episode in 1998.

Although the show generally took place in New York City, in the final program the main characters supposedly got themselves in trouble with Massachusetts law when they failed to help a carjacking victim. (Actually, as we know, there is no duty to rescue law in Massachusetts.) Their defense was: You don't have to help anyone in America, the land of individual freedom.

Is that true? Is that the nation we are? The nation we want to be?

When Kitty Genovese was murdered in 1964 while her neighbors listened and watched and did nothing, even police veterans were shocked. How could "good people," they wondered, have failed to call the police?

Even those "good people" seemed baffled by their own actions. When reporters asked why they didn't try to help, one woman said simply, "I don't know." Stranger still is the neighbor who said that it was difficult to see what was happening in the street because of the light she had turned on in her bedroom. So, she said, "I put out the light and was able to see better." But she didn't call. Another confessed, "I didn't want my husband to get involved."

Not wanting to get involved is a reason used by many witnesses who refuse help to those in danger. And, in truth, the reason has some validity—in certain situations. No one, especially untrained or inexperienced people, should involve themselves in a dangerous situation when they are unlikely to help the victim and stand a good chance of being harmed or killed themselves. But in many cases, all one has to do is make a phone call.

In explaining why she and her husband hadn't called police during the attack on Kitty Genovese, one of Genovese's neighbors said, "We thought it was a lover's quarrel." Does that imply that if people know each other, especially if they are man and woman, violence can be excused? Does that mean it's okay to interfere in a physical struggle only if you think the

The wreckage of the car in which England's Princess Diana and her boyfriend Dodi Fayed were traveling when their chauffeur lost control and slammed into the wall of a tunnel. Duty to rescue issues were again in the news after the 1997 accident when it was learned that photographers who had been chasing the car failed to render assistance to the victims.

people are strangers? Actually, people sometimes believe that. Not long ago two women were walking on a street in Chicago. A man, later discovered to be mentally unbalanced, began walking along with them. Although they tried to ignore him, the man would not go away. Suddenly he grabbed one of the women by the arm and threw her to the ground. She struggled for a few moments as her companion screamed for help. It seemed ages before the owner of a nearby stationery store and his assistant came running out and pulled the man away. Later the store owner apologized to the woman by saying, "I'm sorry. I would have run out sooner to help, but I thought he was your husband."

That feeling of not wanting to interfere in a domestic issue has been deeply ingrained in American life. It is at the root of the problem in charges of domestic abuse. For years police and neighbors tended to treat cases of wife battering as a "family affair," a matter in which strangers should not become involved. Only in recent years has this tendency started to change. Today people are being urged to at least call the police if they suspect their neighbor is being beaten by a partner.

Until recently, when New York City police were called to a scene of wife battering, they would often leave the batterer at home if both parties claimed "the fight was over and everything was okay." That is no longer police policy. If a call is made and battering is suspected, the batterer will be taken into custody and the charges examined—no matter what.

As we've seen, the issue of duty to rescue and Good Samaritan laws is not quite as simple as it may seem. Although all 50 states have some sort of Good Samaritan statute on the books, only 4 tackle the duty to rescue issue. It's a slippery slope.

Beginning in the 1990s, local governments in particular have looked for ways to lower the crime rate. One popular strategy has been to promote community projects, to get people working together to help themselves. In addition to such groups as the Guardian Angels, residents who live on a certain block or in the same apartment building have set up so-called community patrols. Participants may be thought of as volunteer Good Samaritans who take turns walking the block or the halls, on the lookout for fire, vandalism, break-ins, or other crimes. Community patrols have had great success in many cities and smaller towns all across the country. They get people involved in their own protection, and they bring neighborhoods and neighbors closer together.

But what can one person do? What is the right

thing to do if you witness an emergency that puts another person in serious danger? First and foremost, remember that no one expects, and no law requires, you to put yourself in harm's way to rescue another person. Anyway, would that make sense? Would getting yourself hurt help to rescue anyone?

But what if you feel that helping someone in danger is the right thing for you to do? Perhaps the best advice is the advice that professionals give. Don't try to help physically if by doing so you would endanger your own life. Don't jump into water to save a drowning person if you can't swim. Don't run into a burning building to save someone unless you have been trained to do so. Don't think you can stop a shooting by getting in the line of fire. This is just common sense. And being a Good Samaritan means using common sense. If you witness a crime, an accident, or another tragedy, *call the authorities* as soon as you can. That is the right thing to do; it's also the best thing to do.

As we know, there is no nationwide law concerning a duty to rescue. But that may be changing. One person trying to change the way America views the duty to rescue is attorney Charles S. Adubato of New Jersey. His client is a mildly retarded, 23-year-old man who, on January 30, 1999, was kidnapped from his job at a McDonald's restaurant in Tinton Falls, New Jersey. His abductors, nine men and women, took the victim to a nearby apartment in Keansburg, beat and kicked him, forced him to drink alcohol, and subjected him to other indignities and possible sexual abuse. Other attacks may have occurred earlier at various towns and woods in the area.

During the January 30 attack, at least five bystanders watched the abuse of the victim and did nothing. The nine abductors were charged with the crime, but as there is no duty to rescue law in New Jersey, the five witnesses faced no legal consequences.

Adubato intends to change that. He has filed a suit

in Freehold (N.J.) State Superior Court against all 14 of those involved, the 9 charged with the crime and the 5 do-nothing witnesses. Adubato believes that the witnesses could have, and certainly should have, alerted police with no risk to themselves.

"Suing them could break new legal ground," he says. "No court that I know of has been asked to accept civil action in what I'm referring to as bystander liability."

Perhaps this case will break new legal ground concerning our duty to rescue and our status as Good Samaritans. Perhaps the suit against New Jersey's silent witnesses signals a new direction. Will bystander liability make us more aware of how we react to a neighbor in trouble in the 21st century? Time will tell.

Further Reading

Fogelman, Eva. *Conscience and Courage*. Two Harbors, Minn.: Anchor Books, 1994.

Fremont, David. *Holocaust Heroes*. Springfield, N.J.: Enslow, 1998.

Haskins, James. *Guardian Angels*. Hillside, N.J.: Enslow, 1983.

Itaba, Robert. *Courageous Crime-fighters*. Minneapolis: Oliver Press, 1998.

Kenney, Dennis. *Crime, Fear and the New York City Subways*. New York: Praeger, 1987.

Marston, Hope. *To the Rescue*. New York: Cobble Hill, 1991.

Read, Piers Paul. *The Story of the Heroes and Victims of Chernobyl*. New York: Random House, 1993.

Rittner, Carol, and Sondra Myers. *The Courage to Care*. New York: New York University Press, 1982.

Sliwa, Curtis. *Street Smart*. Reading, Mass.: Addison-Wesley, 1982.

Index

Index

ROSE BLUE, an author and educator, has written more than 50 books, both fiction and nonfiction, for young readers. Her books have appeared as TV specials and have won many awards. A native New Yorker, she lives in the borough of Brooklyn.

CORINNE J. NADEN, a former U.S. Navy journalist and children's book editor, also has more than 50 books to her credit. A freelance writer, she lives in Tarrytown, New York, where she shares living quarters with her two cats, Tigger and Tally Ho!

AUSTIN SARAT is William Nelson Cromwell Professor of Jurisprudence and Political Science at Amherst College, where he also chairs the Department of Law, Jurisprudence and Social Thought. Professor Sarat is the author or editor of 23 books and numerous scholarly articles. Among his books are *Law's Violence, Sitting in Judgment: Sentencing the White Collar Criminal,* and *Justice and Injustice in Law and Legal Theory.* He has received many academic awards and held several prestigious fellowships. He is President of the Law & Society Association and Chair of the Working Group on Law, Culture and the Humanities. In addition, he is a nationally recognized teacher and educator whose teaching has been featured in the *New York Times,* on the *Today* show, and on National Public Radio's *Fresh Air.*

Picture Credits